This page is left intentionally blank

A Guide to becoming the best version of you EVER

Shawanna Kennedy

The Power Of Putting YourSELF First

A Guide to becoming the best version of you EVER

Shawanna Kennedy

First Printing, 2017

ISBN 978-0-9987745-2-7

Kennedy Media Entertainment Publishing
http://theselffirstmovement.com/

For information contact:

Kennedy Media Entertainment Publishing
1425 Market Blvd Suite 530-236
Roswell GA. 30076 theselffirstmovement@gmail.com
Book and Cover design for Kennedy Media Entertainment Publishing
First Edition: August 2017

10   9   8   7   6   5   4   3   2   1

DEDICATION

*To my adoring Grandmother Ms. Margaret Emerson
Walker, for her life and the legacy she left. She was a strong woman who lived a life
enriched with the fruit of the spirit. Filled with faith in God and wisdom, her firm
support enabled her family to stand tall! and she gave
me my beautiful Mom Yay...
Ms. Christine Owens...love you!
Thank you to God my Creator, for LIFE and
ALL that you have given taken away denied and allowed. For every thought, you gave in
uniquely designing ME just as
"I Am"
To LaBraun, Shane'a, Gaven
& Elle Jai My sunshine. supporting
and loving me teaching and forgiving me and allowing me to constantly grow.
To All of you who contribute to my life experiences through encouragement support and
prayers, "I Am" forever grateful and stronger because of you.*

*Special Thank you Mr. Hayes for being a mentor and seeing the vision which will bring
great impact to those who embrace it and move to action in their own lives. Excited about
greater things to come.*

TABLE OF CONTENTS

The Introduction

The power of putting yourself first

When or if you have ever flown before, hopefully, you were paying attention to the flight attendants speech before take-off. There is a statement in the speech that could very well be "life-saving" or if not complied with, the situation could also be "life-threatening". The reality of it all is that you and only you get to make that choice. Thus, the power, your power to take care of yourself first.

In life there really should not be any failures only learning; because when we do not learn from shortcomings or less desirable experiences the benefit is the wisdom that one should gain. Scripture refers to the one who does not learn in this instance as a fool. You fail or pass relative to things or projects you attempt to do. In life, the only failure is the refusal to learn. Therefore, the choices we make determine whether we are either wise or foolish.

With this in mind, the author, Shawanna Kennedy has put together a guide to help the reader understand the need for a personal transformation of priorities. The adaptation of this perspective centers around one's capacity to comprehend and embrace the fact that you are the most important part of your world. Whether your mission is to save the world or simply to give life to it; your quest cannot be accomplished without the prioritization that allows you to accept the perspective derived from The "SelfFirst Movement".

The gift here is that Shawanna Kennedy has allowed herself to be vulnerable in sharing with us a glimpse of her life experiences that have helped her to totally embrace this mentality. She has been to a very dark and what she initially thought as a hopeless place in her life.

She will share with us how one can wake up and come to the realization that life basically begins and ends with you. Remember, your account to the creator is based on how did you live; not how others lived. Did you maximize you? Did you take care of you so that you could help others?

Did you honor your gift of choice?

We live in a world overwhelmed with stereotypes; especially that of the woman; i.e. domesticated, homemaker, primary child-raiser, in the kitchen, etc.... For the most part, this is simply considered world ignorance now; given the price that was paid by pioneers before us. The stereotype is and should be a thing of the past in this modern day and therefore not the real issue. The challenge is when we allow others to place us in these boxes of limitation and exclusion due to a subliminal conditioning that says take care of everyone but yourself.

Consequently, the impact is devastating and causes fatigue, exhaustion, low self-esteem and inferior mindset relative to the thought of self. Yes, sometimes we have to be selfish pertaining to our time, health and well-being. This is a perspective that should encourage us to recondition our mentality; understanding that to be selfish is often a prerequisite for the capacity to be selfless.

Hopefully, you can respect that regardless of gender, race or circumstance, this business of tending to everything else but self can lead us down a path of destruction with a run-down nearly worthless remain of yourself. Self-worth is the key. It's the driver and the gage of value. We all are usually driven by how we feel.

How do you feel about you? When you feel that something is of great value, you treat it as such; with care, nourishment, and protection. Embrace your worth and others will come to know your value. No need to let the well run dry. Just value it while it's full and it will never run dry.

It has been said that continuing to do the same things over and over again, yet expecting a different result is the definition of insanity. The irony begins when we start scratching our heads wondering what's wrong and why things keep going in the same empty direction. It's a similar scenario when we question our own shortcomings, yet knowing that we are running ourselves ragged on behalf of others. As a result, we become ill, incapable and inadequate; which makes us non-resourceful and useless to those benefactors. On the contrary, others have become prosperous at your expense and you have become useless.

In turn, they move on to take advantage of another foolish resource (someone else).

The optics here may seem harsh. However, the message is authentic and can help save your life and in turn, save others. The more favorable reality is that if your goal in life is to help others then start by helping yourself first. Accordingly, you will reach that goal in abundance. When you are significantly involved in the life of others with the good intent it is a blessing to them and has to be in divine order.

The divine message here is that everything is sanctioned or ordained by the Creator. Whether one believes that or not, it doesn't really matter. It's just that when something is not working in compliance with your effort to help others; there is no need to scratch your head. Just acknowledge that you are not taking care of you. Thus, the consequence.

I feel that we are all very fortunate for this sharing and therefore responsible to adapt and comply. What's the worst that can happen? A better you of course.   I think we all can live with that. Be wise and take advantage of the learning. Here's to all. Enjoy and be enlightened.

Thank you, Shawanna Kennedy. Your message is clear, and your movement is alive.

By: C. V. Matthew Hayes

3

Putting Yourself First: Why I wrote this book

I can't recall my pre-teen years without images of abuse, pain, and rejection. In my desperation to stop the molestations, I began to binge-eat to intentionally gain weight. My thoughts were that if I appeared unattractive enough, my predator(s) and the molestations would stop. But things appeared to worsen. My self-esteem plunged to an all-time low not to mention spending those formative years and primary stages of development suffering with a lack of self-confidence. It definitely came as no surprise due to the ups and downs of excessive weight gain, and constant pain I became a mother at age nineteen. How could I bring something so beautiful into such an ugly world? I often wondered. But I survived by God's grace.

I recall thinking one particularly bad day: despite these struggles and hellish experiences, if I'd gone through all this without losing my life without losing my mind, I must exist for a purpose bigger than me. It is often said: the more difficult a journey, the greater the responsibility that it leads to. I believed this for myself with every strength in me. I also believe this about everyone who is going through any issues that are and can be destroying their lives right now and can't seem to find a way out.

This was the birthstone of the iAffirm Impact Foundation Non- Profit 501c3 Organization that I am the Founder of and it was established to assist youth of all ages who suffers as I did with low self-esteem and a lack of self-confidence. The SelfFirst Movement is for those individuals who knowingly or unknowingly place everything and everyone on earth before themselves.

My hope is that in these words, you will find peace and healing. Amid my difficulties, I learned to put myself first and to love and affirm myself; I put myself back on my life's to-do list. Not because I had some personal ambition of glory but, burning deep in my heart was a passion to be the best of myself for the sake of the people that I was responsible for and those I believed I would be responsible for in the future through my ministry.

As you read this book, it is my heart's desire that you experience God's grace that will strengthen you on the inside, despite whatever you are going through right now. May your path be lit with uncommon inspiration in periods of deepest darkness and may you begin a mindset shift of empowerment beyond belief and the place people have called your graveyard become your birthing stone.

Shawanna Kennedy SelfFirst Advocate

Chapter 1

Lead Your Life FIRST

The essence of life is being essential or of value to others. And we can only be of value to others to the degree we love ourselves.

A massive tank truck was purchased, and the proud owner quickly filled its huge cylindrical tank with gasoline, anxious to drive off and deliver his load to the next city where great profit awaited him. However, to his greatest shock, the tanker engine refused to start!

He tried everything he could possibly think of, but that tanker wouldn't budge. So, he hired a mechanic who did a few checks and then opened the fuel tank of the vehicle. It was empty.

You have filled the tank on top the truck with enough gasoline to supply a city but you haven't filled the tanker's own engine with fuel to get it to the city which is the first thing you should have done.'

Think of this scenario for a second. A tanker was equipped with sufficient gasoline for a city but was useless to that city because it couldn't deliver that gasoline. And it could not deliver the gasoline because its own fuel tank was empty.

There is a deep lesson in this powerful illustration: We as humans are often like that tank truck. We may be so invested in trying to meet the needs of others that we fail to notice how depleted of health, fresh insight or self-worth we are. The price for not putting our needs first is a loss of time and resources, and ultimately failure. It costs us more not to put ourselves first.

A young man was motivated to make a significant career change that would bring him immense satisfaction and success. However, his girlfriend was concerned he would have less time for her if he took that career change. He put her concerns first and didn't take the career change opportunity. It felt beautiful at first that he had made such sacrifice for his girlfriend.

However, he realized a deep dissatisfaction from missing this opportunity. This dissatisfaction drove such a wedge in their relationship that they eventually broke up. Putting ourselves first must be a means to an end, not the end. The essence of life is being essential or of value to others. And we can only be of value to others to the degree we love ourselves.

Leaders put themselves FIRST so that their legacy will LAST; they position themselves at the head of the journey ahead and inspire their followers from the experiences and successes they as leaders have already first experienced. They climb the mountain first and then pull others up after them.

Action Steps

Learn to tell yourself: I am a beautiful person of value. I am not
motivated by selfish decisions that do not ultimately enrich the
lives of others. I invest value first in myself, so I can be of
better value to others.

_____

_____

_____

_____

_____

_____

Chapter 2

Finding A New Start

We may not be able to reclaim the loss, undo the damage or reverse the consequences but we can ALWAYS make a new start

Why is it so hard for a lot of us to place our needs before the needs of others?

That is the kind of question that comes to mind when one thinks of the story of Sue (not her real name).

She had a brother in law who committed suicide due to drug abuse-related depression. Soon she realized that her own husband was heading down the same self- destructive path as his brother. He couldn't meet her needs or that of their kid. The burden of taking care of her toddler, their stretched finances, and her husband fell entirely on her shoulders.

As a result, she barely had time for her emotional and physical health which were suffering during the process. Her appetite disappeared and her outlook on life became totally negative as she believed only the worst would result from all she was experiencing.

You can't keep this up forever!' Her friend said. 'You are bound to break down at some point. Then, who will take care of you or the people you are taking care of?

Does Sue's story sound like yours?

Then I have got some great advice for you. You don't need to feel guilty or irresponsible about putting yourself first. Learn to put yourself FIRST and this will be the start of a new, beautiful chapter of your life.

Perhaps you used to be an incredibly passionate, motivated and caring person. Perhaps in trying to be responsible for others at your expense, you experienced heartbreak, pain, and failure. I'm here to say: Never use failure as an excuse for not trying again. We may not be able to reclaim the loss, undo the damage or reverse the consequences but we can ALWAYS make a new start!

Don't give up on those dreams and goals that failure may have made you lose sight of. You can embrace them again but with a new approach and with knowledge.

You will be Uplifted Enlighten Encouraged Empowered and Motivated to actions towards being your best Self and feeling very satisfied with the quality of your life to "Put you back on the to-do list of your life" There is still plenty of time to reflect on the beautiful journey this guide provides with relevant probing questions and helpful action steps to take.

You will be glad to know that Sue's story does not end on a sad note. In fact, it does end very beautifully! She is one inspiring individual that discovered the power of putting herself first to reclaim her life.

Action Steps

Begin by setting new personal goals that get you excited. Or you can rediscover personal goals that have been abandoned.

(Later in this guide, we will look at the power of goal setting in the discovering the power of putting yourself first.)

_____

_____

_____

_____

_____

_____

Chapter 3

Origins of putting YourSelf First

Most women have a long generational history of their female needs being purposely denied or suppressed through chauvinism and patriarchy

Let's examine some crucial questions: Why do people believe that they should place themselves last on their list of priorities? Why do people, especially women, have an inbuilt tendency to put themselves last?

There are so many stories about people (especially women), highly intelligent and successful who are in this trap. One expects that they would know better but once its family members or close friends asking for their help, for some reason their own personal needs and best interests take second place. Somehow the needs of others seem more pressing and more important than their own needs.

Why is this a popular trend especially among women? Here are some reasons:

1. Most women have a long generational history of their female needs being purposely denied or suppressed through chauvinism and patriarchy. Women have grown used to being seen as and seeing themselves as second- class members of the society, as far as needs are concerned. This is the sad truth.

2. Age-long traditions, with deep roots in a lot of religions, have supported the belief that a woman's needs - or even value - are inferior when it comes to the family and that a woman's number one responsibility is making certain of her family's wellbeing, at the expense of her own needs.

These are some key reasons why a lot of women embrace a subservient role when it comes to the needs of others. The trend is less popular with the male folk but where a man exhibits this same attitude, it is usually the result of faulty religious traditions that support the belief of putting one's self last.

Thankfully, there are numerous initiatives and corrective measures aimed at these faulty systems of belief. But sadly, these limiting beliefs are still very much an integral part of how our society functions. When we empower ourselves with the truth about our personal value and worth, we are equally empowered to help others realize their own value and worth.

In the next chapter, we will look at some of the myths or false beliefs about putting yourself first, which have come from these faulty origins.

Action Steps

If you are a single person with plans to raise a family, decide right now that those faulty beliefs about women and putting one's self-last will not transfer to your children. Commit to finding a man/woman that treats you as an equal.

If you are married with children, you still have this opportunity to correct faulty beliefs about the importance of one's needs. The rest of this book is dedicated to correcting such faulty beliefs.

_____

_____

_____

_____

_____

_____

Chapter 4

Myths about putting You First

It is hard for us to place our needs before others because of fear.

Let's go back to the first question that was asked in the first chapter: Why is it so hard for a lot of us to place our needs before the needs of others?

We will look at the story of Sue again to gain some insights to this question.

She was afraid that she would lose her husband to drug abuse-related suicide, like her brother in law. Driven by fear, she tried all she could to save her husband from suicide, while trying to maintain stable finances and raise her child.

So, the reason it is hard for us to place our needs before others are because of fear. We are afraid for a number of reasons. And I call these reasons myths. Myths are popular ideas that are false. Some of these myths include:

1. The fear that we are being selfish and irresponsible by putting ourselves first

Some of us believe that we must always sacrifice for others, even at our personal expense. Therefore, we think we are being selfish whenever we put them first. We feel irresponsible and guilty; we feel that if things start to go wrong, we will be criticized by our friends and family for neglecting others that need our help.

2. The fear of failure

Some of us believe that if we are not personally responsible for the needs of others that those people will fail or experience misfortune. We live in fear of how our loved ones will suffer without our help. This was the exact experience of Sue, who thought her husband may kill himself on someday when she wasn't paying attention!

3. The fear of losing our value

Some of us become afraid that others will no longer love us if we don't put them first. So, we continuously look for ways to sacrifice more and more for those people we value so that they can keep on loving us in return.

This is a hard truth: When you put others first at your expense, you are telling them that they are more valuable than you are! In the end, we lose their respect and appreciation. Do you know why? Because people value us as much as we value ourselves.

I've got some powerful words for you: Stop allowing fearful thoughts to create emotions that cause you physical and mental harm! Stop allowing the issues of others consume YOU! Remember you are the protector of your peace and you have control over how your life turns out.

Action Steps

Put yourself back on your to-do-list as number one. List a personal development step you must make FIRST every day before you attend to any other person. It may mean waking earlier or sleeping later but decided to start doing this. Perhaps it might be an exercise, an online course or a skill. Start a journal and write down daily how taking up this personal development skill helps you.

_____

_____

_____

_____

_____

_____

_____

Chapter 5

Putting YourSELF First

Helping others is important, but helping ourselves so that we can keep assisting others is more important

Putting yourSELF FIRST means doing things for yourSelf before doing things for other people.

It does not mean entirely neglecting the concerns of others for our purposes. It does not mean that people become less important or that you care less for them. It simply means putting yourSelf as number one on the to-do list of our life. There are several reasons why this is important:

1. People value and respect us as much as we value and respect ourselves

We, therefore, must cultivate a healthy sense of self-value and self-respect. This is the foundation of putting yourSelf first. If people don't value or respect us, they will not value or respect whatever sacrifices we make for them. It is the cold truth.

2. We can destroy ourselves in the process of always putting people first

In putting others first before our own needs, it's all too easy too soon run into health and emotional problems from self-neglect. Again, we re-visit a key question: Who will take care of you and the ones you care about if you break down from the stress of self- neglect? Helping others is important, but helping yourSelf so that you can keep helping others is more important.

A lady who did a lot of free work for her family and friends in addition to her own full-time work was stuck in a self-destructive pattern: She would work till she broke down physically and required urgent medical attention. During the recovery period, she would lose both finances and valuable time for personal development. After recovering, she would repeat the same process of overworking herself.

A lot of people had her to thank for great things that had happened to them but for her, her life was a mess. She began to exercise, eat much better and began switching off her phone at hours she needed rest. She got into a relationship with someone that took loads of work off her hands. Because she started taking care of herself well, the quality of her service to others improved greatly and with more consistency.

It won't be a popular idea with many people when you tell them you have decided to put yourself first but this is a necessary move. With your knees shaking and teeth chattering, like Nike, Just Do It! Put you back on the list of your life and change your world FOREVER!

Action Steps

Inform the people that will be affected by your decision about your new decisions. Your decision may mean, for example, limiting how often you host dinner for your friends because you need to spend more time at the gym or save money for a holiday. Explain this new development to your friends.

_____

_____

_____

_____

_____

_____

_____

Chapter 6

How to Make Time for You

Your journey to becoming your best self in order to live full and still be of service to others begins by asking YOURSELF uncomfortable questions

Let's go back to our story about Sue.

The wake-up call for Sue to re-consider the focus she gave to her life and her responsibility to others came when her friend said: 'You can't keep this up forever! You are bound to break down at some point. Then, who will take care of you or the people you are taking care of?

Firstly, your journey to becoming your best self in order to live full and still be of service to others begins by asking YOURSELF such uncomfortable questions as Sue's friend asked. Such questions include the following:

Who will take care of you or the people you are taking care of if you break down?

Do the people you sacrifice so much for appreciate your efforts or take you for granted?

What is the quality of results you get from investing all your strength in others?

What do you really benefit from running yourself down to make sure others are doing well?

Secondly, prioritize! Let's start now: Take those goals you wrote down in chapter one. Revise them if you have to until they rekindle passion and motivation and excitement in you. Now ask yourself 'Do you deserve satisfaction through accomplishing these goals? 'YESSSSS!! YOU DESERVE IT!!'

This may feel a bit weird or even strange but welcome to the new you. I need you to begin being OK to say NO to anything that moves you away from these goals. And I need you to start saying 'Yes' to anything that moves you towards these goals! Cut Off Distractions. Distractions may be friends or events that make you feel guilty for focusing on your goals.

Stop the voice in your head and those around you that feed your guilt. As you push towards your goals, soon those accusing voices will become so faint you won't even notice them anymore. Put you back on the list of your life so you can LIVE and not just exist. Don't just be a survivor but a THRIVER.

There are not enough hours in the day to give you what you might have missed out on but, you can MOVE to ACTION now. You are amazing, and it is time you create goals that give purpose and stimulate your soul.

Action Steps

Make a commitment now to be a DOER; do something every day, at every moment you get to move you towards your goals.

Chapter 7

Putting Yourself First: final points

You cannot save everyone. You cannot meet all the needs of everyone you care about. But you can save YOUR own life

Through the course of this book, the truth of what it means to put yourself first, the myths about putting yourself first and the origins of the 'put yourself last' ideas have been looked at. By now you must know one powerful, important fact is: You cannot save everyone. You cannot meet all the needs of everyone but, you can save YOUR own life.

You can take responsibility for your life. When you invest time in yourself, in your mental and emotional health, in your total wellbeing, you find it much easier to support other people. As we begin the journey to be the very best of ourselves by putting our needs first, there are a few points to pay attention to:

We do for others as we expect them to do for us BUT, we don't do for others expecting them to return the favor... as we develop confidence in putting ourselves first and create a balance in the help we give to others, the people who benefit from our personal sacrifice will not always reciprocate our kind, sacrificial gestures. The old you might have been worried or depressed, wondering if what we did was valuable at all to these people.

The old you might have been driven to sacrifice some more, hoping to gain their love and affection. This is known as people-pleasing and this is not selfless at all because people pleasers expect others to please them in return with approval or reciprocal kindness. BUT you are no longer this old person.

You no longer 'let people who do so little for you control so much of your mind, feelings, and emotion' (in the words of Will Smith). The new you have a healthy self- esteem and understands the value of the service you invest in others – you don't need the validation or approval of others to make you feel good about your sacrificial acts of kindness.

Lastly, give yourself time and space to grow

You will make mistakes as you discover a life of putting yourself first. You may sometimes be haunted by guilty feelings when you choose to respond to your needs than the needs of someone else who requires your help. This is why you must keep reminding yourself about why you started to put yourself first in your decisions.

Frame your personal goals in a place you can always see them. Think of what your friends and family will benefit from the best version of you! This will always provide a positive emotional boost for you. Don't Stop and Never Give Up on YOU!

Begin to "MOVE to ACTION" today and you can start by giving yourSELF a BIG hug then lifting both hands... with one waving "Goodbye" to old and wave "Hello" to the new more fulfilled you.

Action Steps

Begin every day with a reminder of why you put yourself first and why you are currently pursuing your personal goals. Remind yourself of all the people that will benefit positively from you being your best self ever!

_____

_____

_____

_____

_____

_____

_____

This page is left intentionally blank

Scripture Reference

(for chapters 1-7 just for you)

Chapter 1

Remember: The price for not putting our needs first is a loss of time and resources, and ultimately failure. It costs us more not to put ourselves first. Here are scriptures that clearly outline the importance of putting our personal development first before that of others.

1 Timothy 4.16: Pay close attention to your life and your teaching; persevere in these things, for by doing this you will save both yourself and your hearers.

Mark 12.31: The second is this: 'Love your neighbor as yourself.' There is no commandment greater than these. " And we can only be of value to others to the degree we value and love ourselves.

Become a PRIORITY in your Life!

Chapter 2

Never use failure as an excuse for not trying again. We may not be able to reclaim the loss, undo the damage or reverse the consequences but we can ALWAYS make a new start! Here are scriptures that encourage you to embrace resilience despite failure and defeat.

Philippians 4:13 I can do all things through Christ who strengthens me. Don't yield to failure; you have assured success if you learn to depend on the grace of Christ

Proverbs 24:16a For the righteous falls seven times and rises again If you are a believer,

you are PROGRAMMED to succeed; failure is not in your nature. In the same way, a rubber foam cannot remain submerged, so you cannot stay down.

Why? Failure is not a part of your divine DNA. Get back up!

Chapter 3

Confront those old-time traditions and false beliefs about your worth as a person. And how do you do that? Two scriptures give us insight:

2 Corinthians 10:4 We use God's mighty weapons, not worldly weapons, to knock down the strongholds of human reasoning and to destroy false arguments. We confront myths and false beliefs about your worth with the word of God.

Embrace what the bible says about you and not what history says about you. Whenever a voice whispers that you are inferior to someone else, confidently declare the word of God that says otherwise.

Colossians 2:8 See to it that no one takes you captive through philosophy and empty deceit, according to human tradition, according to the elemental spirits of the world, and not according to Christ. Secondly, AVOID people who contradict what you believe about your self-worth.

Chapter 4

The reason it is hard for us to place our needs before others are because of fear. But this is the perspective of the Bible.

2 Timothy 1:7 God has not given us a spirit of fear but of love, of power and a sound mind. When you keep confessing that you are not under the control of fear but divine love, soon enough your motivations and outlook will flow from genuine love and not fear.

Psalm 94:19 When worries threaten to overwhelm me, your soothing touch makes me happy. Secondly, learn to live in the consciousness of God's love for you. Remind yourself daily of this.

Chapter 5

People value and respect us as much as we value and respect ourselves. We, therefore, must cultivate a healthy sense of self- value and self-respect. David expressed the awareness of his value and self-worth when he wrote:

Psalm 139:14 I will praise You, for I am fearfully and wonderfully made. Imagine thinking about yourself and saying: Wow! I am so beautiful and precious. Pay attention to the details when it comes to you. You are too valuable not to invest time in knowing your worth.

Ephesians 2:10 For we are God's masterpiece. A masterpiece is a work of outstanding artistry, skill, or workmanship. You and I are God's masterpiece, not others alone. Treat yourself to the level of attention you deserve.

Chapter 6

Your journey to becoming your best self in order to live full and still be of service to others begins by asking YOURSELF 'uncomfortable' questions like do those you place before yourself place equal value on you? Who will take care of them and you if you break down? The Bible invites us to a life of retrospection and foresight regarding our decisions and commitments.

Luke 14:28 But don't begin until you count the cost. For who would begin construction of a building without first calculating the cost to see if there is enough money to finish it? Count the cost. Will neglect your needs for so long have an adverse effect on your life, for example? Decide immediately on what to do about that. Secondly, we saw the need to prioritize our needs.

1 Timothy 3:5 For if someone does not know how to manage his own household, how will he care for God's church? In the same token, if someone cannot manage himself, how will he take care of others? That is why we must come first in our list of priorities

Chapter 7

Sometimes it is, in fact, necessary to put the needs of others before your own but never do so with resentment or reluctance.

2 Corinthians 8:12 For if the willingness is there, the gift is acceptable according to what one has, not according to what one does not have. When we choose to help others, there must be willingness or else or help is of no value. A second verse is even more important

2 Corinthians 8:13, Of course, I don't mean your giving should make life easy for others and hard for yourselves. I only mean that there should be some equality. Never help others to the degree that you suffer. It is NOT biblical.

This page is left intentionally blank

To Do List- START Yours TODAY!

Put you back on the list of your LIFE...

I am going to ...

_____

_____

_____

_____

_____

_____

_____

_____

_____

_____

To Do List!

Put you back on the list of your LIFE...

I am going to....

_____

_____

_____

_____

_____

_____

_____

_____

_____

_____

To Do List!

Put you back on the list of your LIFE...

I am going to....

_____

_____

_____

_____

_____

_____

_____

_____

_____

To Do List!

Put you back on the list of your LIFE...

I am going to....

_____

_____

_____

_____

_____

_____

_____

_____

_____

To Do List!

Put you back on the list of your LIFE...

I am going to....

_____

_____

_____

_____

_____

_____

_____

_____

_____

_____

To Do List!

Put you back on the list of your LIFE...

I am going to....

_____

_____

_____

_____

_____

_____

_____

_____

_____

To Do List!

Put you back on the list of your LIFE...

I am going to....

_____

_____

_____

_____

_____

_____

_____

_____

_____

_____

Author

Shawanna Kennedy is a Transformationalist, The Self First Movement Advocate in addition, the Founder and CEO of the Non-Profit 501c3 iAffirm Impact Foundation. She established iAffirm to build low Self-esteem and Self-confidence to strengthen and empower youth to EMERGE for a better tomorrow.

"Once you know your Worth you know your Worth to the World!"~ Shawanna Kennedy

With an educational background in applied science, music and more than 20 years as a committed woman of faith, Shawanna is able to engage issues with a broad approach, applying timeless principles to individual situations. She does this through a variety of techniques that help even the most challenged to develop greater confidence in themselves and their purpose in life. With that increased confidence, individuals will learn when to say no and when to say yes, to others and to themselves.

Whether individually or in a group setting people begin to benefit from Shawanna's experiences as a confidence coach, speaker, and workshop leader as they shift their mindset from one of depression and limitation to one that recognizes their own self-worth and their place on the list of life. With this new mindset, they find themselves able to work harder and stretch further than ever before.

Bonus Tips

Allow activation to take place and open your heart to you. We have believed the negative NOW, let's give the positive a try. The A.B.C. D's. Of "Selffirst" can change your mindset and by you "Moving to ACTION" and doing things differently to create new habits that will change your world.

A. Allow yourself to change
  **Give yourself permission
B. Believe that it can be done
  **Give yourself this time for you
C. Changed mindset
  **Give yourself a chance to grow
D. Do what's needed and "MOVE to ACTION" and create new habits
  **Give yourself a start to a "Greater" level of knowing YOU!

The BEST project you could ever work on is
YOU! Put You back on the list of your life and win within.

www.theselffirstmovement.com

www.iaffirmimpactfoundation.org

www.facebook.com/shawannaksays

This page is left intentionally blank

This page is left intentionally blank

This page is left intentionally blank

This page is left intentionally blank

www.ingramcontent.com/pod-product-compliance
Lightning Source LLC
Chambersburg PA
CBHW051711090426
42736CB00013B/2652

9 780099 877452 7